12/10

AUG 2 5 2012	DATE DUE	

BL:4.1 AR:0.5 Pt 138037

Donkeys
Jennies, Jacks, and Foals

Lorijo Metz

PowerKiDS press

New York

To Joshua Cincinnati, who possesses the best qualities of a donkey:
strength and intelligence

Published in 2011 by The Rosen Publishing Group, Inc.
29 East 21st Street, New York, NY 10010

First Edition

Editor: Amelie von Zumbusch
Book Design: Greg Tucker
Photo Researcher: Jessica Gerweck

Photo Credits: Cover, pp. 4, 5, 6, 7 (bottom), 8, 9, 10, 13, 16, 19 (bottom) Shutterstock.com; p. 7 (top) © www.iStockphoto.com/Trout55; p. 11 © www.iStockphoto.com/Lynn Graesing; p. 12 © www.iStockphoto.com/Rafal Pellc; p. 12 DEA/G. Dagli Orti/Getty Images; p. 15 © www.iStockphoto.com/Michael Westhoff; p. 17 Monty Rakusen/Getty Images; p. 18 Rainer Grosskopf/Getty Images; p. 19 (top) © www.iStockphoto.com/Todd Lammers; p. 21 © M. Henning/age fotostock; p. 22 © www.iStockphoto.com/Darren Hendley.

Library of Congress Cataloging-in-Publication Data

Metz, Lorijo.
  Donkeys : jennies, jacks, and foals / Lorijo Metz. — 1st ed.
      p. cm. — (On the farm)
  Includes index.
  ISBN 978-1-4488-0688-1 (library binding) — ISBN 978-1-4488-1337-7 (pbk.) — ISBN 978-1-4488-1338-4 (6-pack)
  1. Donkeys—Juvenile literature. I. Title. II. Series: Metz, Lorijo. On the farm.
  SF361.M48 2011   43329
  636.1'82—dc22
  Ingram #15.95   2010001610
  12/10
Manufactured in the United States of America

CPSIA Compliance Information: Batch #WS10PK: For Further Information contact Rosen Publishing, New York, New York at 1-800-237-9932

Contents

Meet the Donkey

Does a donkey look like a small horse to you? If you said yes, there is a good reason for that! Donkeys belong to the same family of animals as horses, ponies, and zebras. They are all **equines**.

Like cattle, sheep, and pigs, donkeys are livestock. Donkeys were one of the last types of livestock to be **domesticated**. Scientists think donkeys were domesticated in Africa over 5,000 years ago.

As all equines do, this donkey has a mane. Donkey manes are shorter and stiffer than horse manes.

People often ride donkeys. This man is riding a donkey to move his flock of sheep.

Over the years, people have used donkeys and their **relatives**, mules and hinnies, for many purposes. However, as you will learn, a donkey's true value lies in its strength and **intelligence**!

Farm Facts

Male donkeys are called jacks. Female donkeys are called jennets or jennies, and baby donkeys are called foals.

These donkeys are feral donkeys. Feral animals are domesticated animals that have gone back to living in the wild.

What Do Donkeys Look Like?

Donkeys stand only 36 to 56 inches (91–142 cm) tall. They are smaller than most horses. However, compared to the size of their bodies, donkeys have larger heads. They also have much longer ears. Donkeys' long ears

As this donkey does, many donkeys have white muzzles. The muzzle is the part of the head that includes the nose and mouth.

keep them cool in hot weather. They are also good for hearing **predators**, such as wolves, from far off. Donkeys have large D-shaped eyes, set on the sides of their heads. These give them a wide view of the world around them.

Donkey coats come in several colors, such as black, gray, and brown. Many donkeys have lighter-colored stomachs, as this one does.

Unlike a horse's coat, a donkey's coat does not guard it from snow, wind, and rain. Donkeys' hooves are smaller and rounder than horses' hooves. However, they are very strong.

In this picture you can see many of the differences between a donkey (right) and a horse (left).

Donkey Foals

Donkeys continue to grow until they are about three years old. By age six, they look and act much as they will through the rest of their lives.

Female donkeys, or jennies, should be at least three years old before they have their first foal. This is because their bones are still growing. Donkeys are

This little donkey is a foal. Donkey foals generally have thick, fluffy coats. Their eyes and ears tend to look big.

Mother donkeys like to stay close to their foals. A mother donkey and her foal should not be apart for more than a few hours. When their mothers are working, donkey foals often walk alongside them.

mammals. Jennies carry their babies for between 10 and 14 months. Most foals are born with their legs coming out first. Newborn donkey foals stand within an hour. For the first six months of their lives, baby donkeys drink only their mothers' milk.

Hee-Haw, the Life of a Donkey!

A donkey's bray is loud. It sounds like "Hee-haw, hee-haw!" In the wild, donkeys bray to let other donkeys know there is water nearby.

Donkeys are much happier if they have companions! They get sad and lonely if they are alone all the time.

It is also a way to tell other donkeys when predators are near! However, braying can also be a sign that a donkey is lonely.

This small donkey herd lives on a farm in Iowa. In the wild, donkey herds are also often small.

Donkeys live in groups, or herds. On farms or as pets, they are happiest in pairs. They can also find **companions** in other livestock or people. Some people think donkeys are stubborn, or want to do things their own way. In truth, donkeys are intelligent and careful. Scared donkeys do not run. They stand still and carefully consider what to do next.

What Do Donkeys Eat?

These three donkeys are eating hay. A bunch of grass and other related plants that have been cut and dried is known as hay.

Compared to other livestock, donkeys cost little to feed. This is because today's domesticated donkeys eat much the same way that wild donkeys did thousands of years ago. Wild donkeys lived in deserts and high places where food was hard to find. They could get water and **nutrients** from food on which other animals could not live.

For the most part, domestic donkeys can live on grass, hay,

Farm Facts

Donkeys can eat plants with thorns. How do they do this? They curl their lips so the thorns will not hurt them.

These donkeys are eating grass. Rich foods are bad for donkeys. It is much healthier for them to eat grass.

and clean water. Donkeys like treats, though, and will gladly eat vegetables, such as carrots. They also need nutrients from salt, which farmers give them in the form of salt blocks.

Donkeys Yesterday and Today

Around 5,000 years ago, people began keeping donkeys for their meat, milk, and **hides**. They soon realized there were better uses for these strong, intelligent animals. Donkeys could handle much of the heavy work on farms, guard livestock, and carry people around. In the 1500s, Spanish **explorers** brought the first donkeys to

This carving from ancient Egypt shows a farmer with his donkeys. In ancient Egypt, donkeys were used to carry goods and to prepare the ground for crops.

This donkey is guarding a group of sheep. Donkeys make good livestock guardians both because they are smart and because they get along well with other farm animals.

what is now the southwestern United States. The **descendants** of these donkeys are known as burros. Burros are generally small.

Today, machines do many of the jobs that donkeys once did. Farmers still use donkeys to guard sheep and goats, though. Donkeys also make good companions and training partners for younger horses and goats.

15

You Think You'd Like a Pet Donkey?

Donkeys love people. Farmers often keep them as pets. Calvin Coolidge, the thirtieth president of the United States, had a pet donkey named Ebeneezer. However, before you buy a pet donkey, there are a few things

Donkeys can make very good pets. Most donkeys are friendly. They like the company of both other animals and people.

you must consider. Donkeys need lots of attention. They should have companions, such as other donkeys or goats. Donkeys need **shelter**, room to **graze**, food,

Donkeys need a lot of care and attention. Caring for your donkey keeps it healthy. It also makes for a stronger tie between you and the donkey.

and plenty of clean water. Their hooves need special care. They also need the services of a **veterinarian** at least once a year. Donkeys can live 40 years or more. You will need to be around to take care of them!

What Is a Mule?

People often mix up mules and donkeys. In fact, the two are closely related. A mule is the child of a donkey father and a horse mother. Though they are larger than them, mules look more like their donkey fathers. Their loud brays

Taking a ride on a mule makes a trip to the already striking Grand Canyon even more memorable.

are a cross between a horse's whinny and a donkey's bray.

People often use mules as pack animals. Like donkeys, they are **sure-footed**, intelligent, and strong. Like their horse mothers, mules tend to be

As you can see here, a mule's face looks a bit like a donkey's and a bit like a horse's.

fearless. This comes in handy when carrying heavy loads and people over steep, rocky ground. For over 100 years, people have trusted mules to carry them safely over the steep trails of the Grand Canyon, in Arizona.

This mule has a saddle on its back and a bridle on its head. It is prepared to carry a rider across trails at Arizona's Grand Canyon National Park.

It's a Hinny!

You might say a hinny is the opposite of a mule. Hinnies have a donkey mother and a horse father. They are generally smaller than mules. Hinnies are also less common. On a farm or even on a trail, you will find hinnies doing much the same work as donkeys and mules.

It can be hard to see the differences between mules and hinnies. In general, a hinny's face looks more like a horse's. A hinny's ears are most often smaller and rounder, too. Hinnies also tend to have the same color coat as their horse fathers'. However, like their donkey mothers, they like to do things slowly and carefully.

Hinnies generally act more like donkeys than horses. However, they are more likely to neigh like a horse than to bray like a donkey.

A Special Place in Our World

Every year, thousands of children enjoy donkey rides on farms and at circuses. Donkeys are still used to get around in some parts of the world, too. For example, riding a sure-footed donkey is still a good way to get around on some rocky islands. Many people who visit these islands on vacation like riding donkeys there, too.

These donkeys are on a beach in Scarborough, Yorkshire, in Great Britain. Kids on vacation take rides on the donkeys.

Donkeys, mules, and hinnies have served people for many years. Their gentle nature, intelligence, and strength have earned them a special place in our world.

Glossary

companions (kum-PAN-yunz) Friends.

descendants (dih-SEN-dents) Animals born of a certain family or group.

domesticated (duh-MES-tih-kayt-id) Raised to live with people.

equines (EE-kwynz) Animals in the horse family.

explorers (ek-SPLOR-erz) People who travel and look for new land.

graze (GRAYZ) To feed on grass.

hides (HYDZ) The skins of animals.

intelligence (in-TEH-luh-jentz) Smartness.

mammals (MA-mulz) Warm-blooded animals that have backbones and hair, breathe air, and feed milk to their young.

nutrients (NOO-tree-unts) Food that a living thing needs to live and grow.

predators (PREH-duh-terz) Animals that kill other animals for food.

relatives (REH-luh-tivz) Animals in the same family.

shelter (SHEL-ter) A place that guards something from weather or danger.

sure-footed (shur-FU-ted) Tending not to fall.

veterinarian (veh-tuh-ruh-NER-ee-un) A doctor who treats animals.

Index

Due to the changing nature of Internet links, PowerKids Press has developed an online list of Web sites related to the subject of this book. This site is updated regularly. Please use this link to access the list:
www.powerkidslinks.com/otf/donkey/